# All Color Book of
# Oriental Carpets and Rugs

## Stanley Reed

Octopus Books

# Contents

First published in the United States of
America in 1972 by Crescent Books,
a Division of Crown Publishers, Inc.,
419 Park Avenue South,
New York, N.Y. 10016

© 1972 Octopus Books Limited

ISBN 0 7064 0170 0

Produced by Mandarin Publishers
Limited, Hong Kong

Printed in Hong Kong

# Introduction

This is a subject which knows no beginning and no end. No beginning, because until a few years ago no proof whatever existed that what we know as Oriental rugs and carpets could have been produced prior to the Christian era, and no end, because such products are still being made today in the same way as in those far off days. Before delving into the historical and technical details of this fascinating subject, it is necessary to define exactly what is meant by an Oriental rug, or carpet. It is true that machine-made carpets and rugs are now manufactured in some parts of the East, particularly Japan, but the definition we are seeking is of a hand-made, knotted product, made in any of the traditional areas between Turkey and China. Some licence must be given, however, to include certain aspects of Balkan production, the early carpets of Egypt, and passing mention of Spain. Also included are the pileless fabrics used as hangings, divan covers or floor coverings, and known by various names, but most popularly as Kelims.

It is also necessary to define what is meant by 'rug' and 'carpet'. Throughout this book the English version of these terms will be used. That is, a rug is any piece smaller than 9ft. × 6ft. From this size upwards the term 'carpet' will be used. There are two exceptions to this rule. A long and narrow piece is a runner, and a carpet of size 12ft. × 6ft. or larger, but in that proportion, is a Kelleye. The reason for this explanation is that in America the term 'scatter rug' is used for small pieces, 'rug' is used for large ones, and carpets refer to machine-made fitted carpeting with which we are not concerned.

## The Historical Background

In view of the comparatively recent discovery of a rug dating from the fifth century BC (now known as the Pazyryk rug), in the wild and mountainous region of Gorny-Altai, it is now believed that the first hand-knotted carpets ever to be woven were made in Persia. Time alone will tell if this is true or not, when some future expedition uncovers more of the treasures of the Old World.

From this time onwards we are left with no actual examples, apart from some fourth century textiles from Egypt, which, although with a form of pile, are not to be classed with the true product, until the thirteenth century—these latter pieces being of Turkish origin. They were taken from the Mosque of Ala-ad-Din in Konia, and are now in the Museum of Islamic Art, in Istanbul. Even here the dating is doubtful.

This is the real beginning of the unbroken history of the craft, for although the next two or three centuries leave us little in the way of rugs themselves, and many of these not fully authenticated, it was an era of pictorial evidence, and countless paintings abound, particularly by Italian and Dutch masters, showing rugs and carpets as decoration either on the floor or thrown over tables. Some rugs have even acquired an artist's name, and one can read of 'Holbein' and 'Lotto' rugs, signifying the design painted by these artists.

Between the time of the Pazyryk and Konia examples stories come down to us of fabulous carpets, particularly through the writings of Marco Polo who, speaking of Asia Minor said, 'The best and handsomest carpets in the World are wrought here, and also silks of crimson and other rich colours'.

Another story concerns the fabulous 'Spring of Chosroes' carpet, from Ctesiphon. This was obviously not a knotted pile carpet as we know it. The size was reputed to be sixty cubits square – a cubit being the length of the forearm from elbow to the end of the middle finger, approximately 1ft. 6in. This would make the carpet about 90ft. × 90ft., a formidable size in any material. Apparently it was woven of silk, the pattern being representative of a garden, with streams, pathways, lawns and trees, the branches and flowers of which were made of precious stones of various colours. The object of the carpet was to create an illusion of spring time during the winter months for King Chosroes. Alas, the Persian Empire fell to the Arab invaders in 637 AD and the famous carpet was carried away to be cut up and divided amongst the conquerors as booty. It is said that several pieces found their way into the Baghdad bazaar. This carpet must have been of tapestry or flat weave type from its description. It is inconceivable to think of a piece of this size, with knotted pile, and bejewelled as well.

Early in the sixteenth century the position became much clearer. Turkey and Persia were producing great quantities of carpets, and some of these were being sent to all parts of the known world – to Egypt, North Africa, Spain, Venice of course, and through this great city to the Continent of Europe and England. Eastwards, the craft spread into India, and to Turkestan and China, although the latter may already have developed the art independently. This state of affairs lasted until the latter part of the seventeenth century, when a general decline set in, and it was not until the middle of the nineteenth century that the art was revived, this time due not to court patronage, but to commercial considerations. Today, once again, production, quality-wise, is at a low ebb, and this time it is possible that the end of the road is in sight. Eventually the hand-knotted product must cease to exist, apart from a few prestige pieces.

Unlike the sculptor or painter who is able to carry his own idea through from conception to finality, the 'carpet maker' is a complex body of people who perform various tasks, some very menial and none completely satisfactory in themselves, and it only needs a breakdown in one function for the whole operation to collapse.

6

# Some Technical Details

The definition of an Oriental carpet or rug is a 'hand knotted product'. Before the hand knotting, however, many processes have to be performed. Wool mainly, and silk rarely, are the chief materials for the pile, whilst either cotton or wool will be needed for the foundation. These raw materials must be sorted, scoured and spun into yarn before the important dyeing procedure. Today, of course, these materials can be purchased already spun, and even dyed to specification, and most of the city-made, and commercially contracted carpets now being produced are made from machine spun yarns. Before this was possible, however, and indeed, in some of the more inaccessible places today, the sheep are locally bred, and every process of manufacture has to be carried out on the spot. All these preparatory processes require great skill, but the weavers are the people who actually produce the end product. However, these weavers are not creative artists in themselves. In the cities and manufacturing centres, even back to the days of court manufacture, they must be guided by designs conceived by artists of the first order and painstakingly drawn upon squared paper—one square for each knot of the carpet. In rural areas and amongst the nomadic peoples other methods of acquainting the weavers with the design formulae are used, such as drawing in the sand, or having the sequence of colours read or sung out to them. With repetition and long experience, especially in the making of pieces with tribal or other distinctive patterns, the weaver can memorize the sequences and at this stage he or she can work alone without the aids mentioned above.

After the weaving, the carpet has to be sheared and washed, usually in local water or at some central point where the properties of the water are known and recommended. The chemical washing process to which certain modern pieces are subjected is done in Western countries to suit the particular taste of the market.

Basically there are two types of knot used throughout the Orient. The Ghiordes or Turkish knot (which is a full knot) and the Senneh or Persian knot (which is a half knot and can be left-handed or right-handed). Strangely enough, although the Pazyryk rug is attributed to Persia it is made with the Ghiordes knot. Another strange fact is that the Senneh rugs of Persia are usually, although not always, made with the Ghiordes knot. It is not known how these names came to be used, and perhaps it would be better if they were called just Turkish and Persian, or full and half knots, leaving the town names out of it altogether.

The dyeing process still involves locally made dyestuffs (of animal and vegetable origin) in some instances, particularly in country districts, but of course, modern synthetic dyes form the major proportion of those used today.

Until the middle of the nineteenth century all dyes were of natural origin, and the secrets of the craft were well guarded by the dye masters. These skills tended to run in families, and the recipes were handed down from father to son. Even after the invention of artificial dyes there was resistance to their use, particularly in Persia, where they were banned until the turn of the century.

# Persia

The art of the Oriental carpet never reached greater heights than those achieved in Persia (or Iran as it is now called) during the Sefavi dynasty of the sixteenth and seventeenth centuries. The rulers of the time, of which the names of Shah Tahmasp and Shah Abbas the Great stand out, were patrons of all the arts, but the carpets produced in this period have never been equalled anywhere. The leading artists of the day were commissioned to design these masterpieces, and the materials used were the finest obtainable. It is still not known where they were actually made; in fact it could be in any of the various cities where the court moved to during the many wars which were being waged during these troubled times.

The cities of Tabriz, Isfahan, Kazvin and Kashan are variously named as their birthplace, but it is more than likely that the carpet manufactory, together with its ancillary departments was carried around with the court as it moved. The few surviving carpets from this period are to be seen in those museums featuring Oriental textile art, but there must have been vast quantities made at the time. After the death of Shah Abbas the Great, the art gradually ceased to be important, and it reached its lowest point with the Afghan invasion of 1721. It did not recover until well into the nineteenth century. The revival was partly due to the interest of the then Shah, who was of the Qajar dynasty, and also to the re-awakening interest of the Western world in the craft. Tabriz became the centre of this revival at first, but it soon involved other towns and villages, and gradually an export business was built up with Tabriz as the main transit centre. Buyers came from all over Europe and America to Tabriz.

Western firms opened offices there and appointed buying agents, whilst local merchants shipped their wares to the markets of the West, and many went with their goods to become dealers in the principal cities of Europe and America. By the end of the nineteenth century a large business had been built up, not with the old traditional, long and narrow pieces, but with special designs and sizes to suit the houses of the new clientele. London became a particularly important transit market, as it still is, with vast warehouses filled with rugs and carpets from all over the Orient. Today's production however, quality-wise, apart from a few prestige pieces is but a shadow of that obtaining at the end of the nineteenth century. That is why the products of that period are so prized when they are found in good condition.

# Turkey

It was the carpets from Turkey which first penetrated into Europe, through Venice, and the sixteenth and seventeenth centuries leave us in no doubt, through the efforts of the artists of the day in Europe, that there must have been a good trade in this commodity. All carpets entering England for instance were called 'Turkey' even though many of them were from other places. There was one notable exception to this. In 1518 Cardinal Wolsey asked the Venetian Ambassador for some 'Damascene' carpets. At that time wines were being imported into England from Candia by the Venetian merchants, and a duty was levied upon them which the

traders were anxious to have repealed. Were Cardinal Wolsey's request to be met, he promised to take the Ambassador before the Council, so that the envoy could argue for the repeal of the duties. Apparently the Cardinal received a few pieces during that year, but they do not seem to have satisfied his appetite, because he proceeded to demand a hundred 'Damascene' carpets in 1519 with the same promise contingent upon them.

Apart from this exception, all carpets, even English made pieces were called 'Turkish', although in the case of the latter, the preserved inventories read 'Turkey carpets of English making'. Carpets also entered Europe through another channel – Spain. Not directly however. They came via North Africa, due to the Moorish conquest of Spain. The Spanish people eventually established the manufacture of carpets in their own right, with Spanish inspired designs, and even a completely different system of knotting from that of the Orient. What is known as the 'Spanish' knot was evolved, and it remains to this day. Basically it is the Ghiordes or Turkish knot, but tied on one warp thread instead of on two. In each row of knots alternate warp threads are used. The Spanish carpet of the last two or three centuries therefore, whilst being Oriental in concept, is quite significantly different from its sister weave.

The earliest rugs of Turkey were of angular design, and many of them may have come from what we now know as the Caucasus. The port of Constantinople (Istanbul) was the clearing house for all the goods being exported to Europe, and there must have been many Caucasian and Persian pieces shipped, which on arrival were just designated as 'Turkish'. Even the famous carpet of the Worshipful Company of Girdlers in London was described in the minutes of the Company as a 'very faire long Turkey Carpitt' but we know it was made in India.

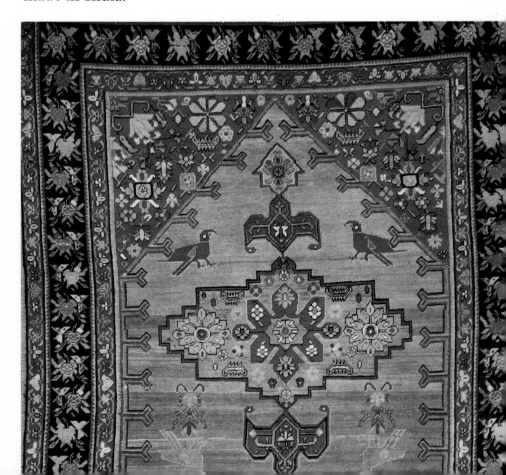

# The Caucasus

The carpet producing parts of Russia are confined to two areas–the Caucasus and Turkestan. The former, sandwiched between the Black Sea and the Caspian, is the home of the pieces made with completely angular designs. No curves are to be found at all. The ornate and formal curvilinear designs developed in Persia in the sixteenth century did not penetrate into this wild, mountainous country. There is no organized manufacture as in Persia, and Turkey, it is purely a cottage and nomadic industry. The only carpets with any formality about them were the Armenian Dragon carpets of the fifteenth and sixteenth centuries. Usually attributed to Kuba, these highly stylized, so-called 'dragon' designed pieces were obviously made for use in houses, being in long and narrow sizes. Very few of these carpets are left, but most of the museums of Europe and America have at least one to show, if they feature Caucasians at all.

Other than this type, there do not appear to be many pieces from the Caucasus in existence dating from earlier than the second half of the eighteenth century, possibly because all their production was purely functional, there being no court production as in Persia, where the highest degree of artistic excellence was attained, for the sake of appearance.

The eighteenth and nineteenth century prayer rugs form the largest part of Caucasian production still in use. Prayer rugs to cover unclean ground are made and used by all people who profess the Moslem faith. They are colourful, extremely well made, and the materials used are first class, for the country is ideal for breeding the hardy sheep that give the tough springy wool which is necessary for floor coverings.

# Western Turkestan – The Bokhara Weaves

Purely functional, with a variety of uses unknown in other parts of the Orient, the weavings of Western Turkestan owe nothing to the professional designer, although the resulting product is invariably a work of art.

Rugs, saddlebags, door hangings, gun covers, cushions, water bottle covers, tent bags and tent bands are just some of the ingenious articles made with hand knotted pile, all the trappings of a nomadic people, and all made for easy transportation during the frequent tribal movements.

In design, all Turkoman pieces have features distinguishing the tribe which made them, for there is no formal manufacture at all, the same designs being handed down through the generations. Historically, the products of this area must stem from a long ancestry, although the subject has never been fully explored. It was, of course, the original home of the Turks, and there is no reason to believe that the knotting art was not taken by them when they moved westwards, eventually to settle in Turkey. Consequently, the craft may have moved to the West rather than from it, as is popularly supposed. The ancient trade route from China passed through Turkestan, and although in neither case have we any direct evidence of early participation in the craft, the eminence of China in most other fields of art makes one think that the art of carpet knotting must have been mastered many centuries ago in that vast country.

Turkestan did not have any real communication with the Western world until after the Russian conquest late in the nineteenth century, and even then the flow of rugs out of the country was not considerable until well into the twentieth century. The nature of these goods, made by a primitive people, for use rather than ornament, and subject to abnormal wear by the very nature of their way of life, makes it impossible to put a date earlier than the beginning of the nineteenth century on any piece. The city of Bokhara is the market for goods being sold, and this name is used throughout the world to describe the products of this remote country. Actually, the tribal name should be used for accuracy, but there are many pitfalls in identification, for even though the tribes have their own motifs, many of these have been copied by other tribes, sometimes through marriage, or have become stylized, and are somewhat difficult to place. The main characteristic of the Turkoman weave is the brown to red ground colour, which is peculiar to this part of the world. It is very appropriate to this wild, cold and inhospitable country. Also usually featured is the motif, in one form or another, popularly known as the 'elephant's foot' design.

# Eastern Turkestan– The Samarkand Weaves

Not very far to the east of Bokhara lies the ancient city of Samarkand. Not a carpet-making centre itself, Samarkand is a collecting centre for the products of the area very much to the east, and into Chinese Turkestan. Collectively known as 'Samarkand', these colourful pieces with both Chinese and Persian influence in them are really made in the vicinity of three important towns–Kashgar, Yarkand and Khotan.

As with Western Turkestan one cannot delve too deeply into the antiquity of these pieces, as there is no direct evidence to work on, but there is no doubt that rugs have been made in this part of the world for a very long time, even though there are no specific examples to show for it. Also, it is possible that instead of coming to the West, the products of this strange country went eastwards to grace the floors and walls of rich Chinese households. It was not until the nineteenth century that what we now regard as Samarkand rugs arrived in Europe. They must have been looked at with disdain, because they were coarse in comparison with the Persian weaves, and they lacked the finesse of the Persian designs. What they lacked in these respects however, were offset by their brilliant colours and complete contrast in configuration.

Commercially they were not a success, and very few people took the trouble to collect them, until the advent of the chemical washing process, when the interior decorators started to use them in their schemes, after the lovely bright colours had been removed, leaving them a wishy-washy shadow of their former beauty. Not only did the wash remove the colours, it also removed the firmness of the piece, and it handled like limp cloth.

Some pieces escaped this punishment, of course, and those now remain with us to illustrate the art of a primitive people, far removed from the civilized world as we know it, living in one of the most inaccessible parts of the world, and surrounded by some of the highest mountains in Asia.

# Egypt–India–Kashmir– China

A craft which, so far as is known, spans a period of nearly 2,500 years, and which is still practised over a large part of the earth's surface, naturally has its areas where development was more pronounced than others; where the evolution of the people led them to greater heights in a particular field of enterprise, and where it was possible, in the age of Western exploration and exploitation, to study, at least superficially, the intricacies and history of the craft. Such is the case of the Oriental rug, and the previous sections have discussed the areas best known and most open to Western study. The remaining areas, well known by name, have not made any significant contribution to the art of knotted textiles, but they have left a legacy of design technique which shows that copying is a two way traffic, and national considerations can over-ride the conquerors' whims, or the imported weavers' ideas. The prime example of national inspiration is Egypt. This country has a long record of textile production stretching back well into the pre-Christian era, but the earliest remains of what could conceivably be classified as knotted fabrics are some fragments of undoubtedly heavy cloth with a form of pile. These date from the fourth century AD. Opinion varies as to whether this fabric was made in the manner of Oriental rugs, or whether it was just a looped cloth rather in the nature of a Turkish towel. Some of the loops are cut, but whether this was done deliberately or through wear is not known.

The first examples of actual carpet knotting however, date from the Mameluke period, and these were made in Cairo. Although they were made with the Senneh or Persian knot, they certainly did not emulate any previously known designs. The nearest approach to these unique pieces would be the Caucasian, but even here the only resemblance was that both were angular in design rather than curvilinear.

The essence of these carpets was a rather indistinct design, usually not conventionally bordered, in three or four colours—red, green, blue, and yellow—giving the appearance of a mosaic rather than a textile fabric. This type of design persisted after the Ottoman conquest of 1517, but gradually the Turkish influence took over, and, no doubt due to the requirements of the Turkish court, the designs became more akin to those of Persia, with rounded forms, medallions, corner pieces and properly constructed borders. These designs, however, could never match the beautiful proportions and exquisite designing of the Persian examples.

For reasons not fully explained, the Cairo carpets have often been designated as 'Damascus'. Perhaps this stems from the demands of Cardinal Wolsey in 1518, who wanted 'Damascene' carpets, and possibly his demand was in perpetuation of the idea that these carpets bore some resemblance to the even then popular fabric known as damask.

There was no gentle decline in Egyptian carpets. There appears to have been an abrupt end to the weaving in the seventeenth century. This could be because the weavers were shipped off to work for their Turkish masters in Constantinople, leaving no more use for the looms of Cairo.

In discussing India it is necessary to include the whole of the sub-continent, including what is now known as Pakistan, and, of course, Kashmir. There is no evidence of carpet manufacture before the Moguls, although they were imported from Persia—particularly Kirman. However, the Emperor Akbar, with the help of Shah Abbas the Great of Persia, acquired Persian weavers, and started a manufactory in India. At first, as can be expected, the Persian designs were copied, and there is a class of carpet from the sixteenth and seventeenth centuries known as Indo-Isfahan, or Indo-Persian. Obviously, these were direct copies of Persian originals, or carpets made from designs prepared by Persian artists. India had, however, some very good schools of design, practising all the arts, and gradually a change took place in carpet design, until a typical Indian design was developed. The centres of weaving were Agra and Lahore. There are not many early pieces left, and most of these cannot be identified with any particular centre of manufacture. The famous Girdlers carpet, however, still in the possession of the Worshipful Company of Girdlers in the City of London, has been well documented and it is recorded as having been made in Lahore.

Kashmir has for centuries been famous for textiles of one kind or another. There are no carpets of antiquity that can be attributed to this area, but a few very fine rugs were made about fifty years ago which for sheer fineness of weave have never been surpassed. The knotting—wool pile on silk warps—is in the order of 2,500/2,600 knots to the square inch. They appear to be scaled down replicas of the classical Persian originals. Whether they were samples, actual carpets for doll's houses, or just extravagant purchases made to order from princely families has never been confirmed. Useless as they are from a practical point of view, they are, however, of such technical importance that they should be preserved for posterity.

Rugs and carpets have probably been made in China for many centuries and records tell us that carpets were being used in 1122 BC, but not a vestige remains to offer any proof. It was the nineteenth century travellers who first brought back any information about the textile products of this vast country, and since that time a considerable industry has grown up to supply the needs of the Western markets. Of the antique pieces still in existence, most of them emanate from Pekin, but they are not as colourful as those pieces attributed to Ningsia and Sinkiang, which are more akin to the products of Eastern Turkestan than to China proper.

# Classical Carpets

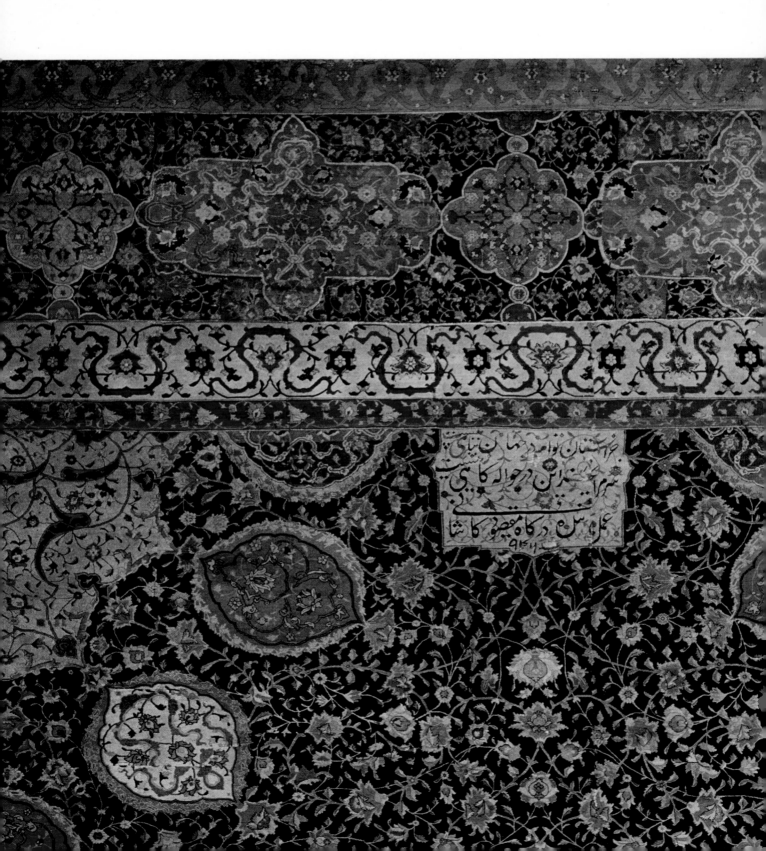

**1 Ardebil Carpet (detail)**

Found in a Mosque in Ardebil, north west Persia, this carpet is one of the finest examples extant of the work carried out during the Sefavi dynasty, the Golden Age of Persian production. The size is 34ft. 6in. × 17ft. 6in. and it is constructed with wool pile on silk foundation, the knotting being Senneh or Persian.

Apart from its beautifully balanced proportions and superb colours the most important feature is the cartouche at one end of the carpet. This reads: *'I have no refuge in the World other than thy threshold. There is no protection for my head other than this door. The work of the slave of the threshold Maksoud of Kashan in the year 946'* This year in the Moslem Calendar corresponds with 1539/40 AD.

2

## 2 The Pazyryk Rug

What has now become known as the first ever hand knotted rug was discovered by the Russian archaeologist S. I. Rudenko during an expedition in 1947–9 to the Pazyryk valley of southern Siberia, a few miles from the Outer Mongolian border, in the region called Gorny Ältai. It was found in a burial mound, together with tapestries, felt wall hangings, chariots and leather work, all preserved by natural refrigeration – perennial ice. The rug is 6ft. 6in. × 6ft. 0in. in size, of fairly fine knotting and is woven with the Ghiordes or Turkish knot. The design is Persian, and many of the motifs can be found in the Persian art of the time, and earlier. A general study of the articles found shows that the contents of the tomb date from the fifth century BC. In addition, the Pazyryk rug has been subjected to a radio-active carbon test with a result within a hundred years of this date.

3

**4**

**5**

### 3 Hunting Carpet (detail)

This is a smaller carpet than the Ardebil, being 18ft. 9in. × 12ft. 0in., but it is signed and dated, and is earlier than the masterpiece in the Victoria and Albert Museum.

There is some controversy as to the correct date owing to the fact that the figures are badly worked into the carpet, but a close study of the cartouche, which is in the centre of the piece, reveals that the most plausible date is 929 AH corresponding to 1523 AD and not 949 AH as some authorities suppose.

### 4 The Chelsea Carpet (detail)

So called because it was acquired by the Victoria & Albert Museum, London, around the beginning of the twentieth century from a dealer in Kings Road, Chelsea, this piece is another of the masterpieces of the world.

The size is 18ft. 0in. × 10ft. 0in. and like most of the other examples of the Sefavi period it is woven on a silk foundation with wool pile. It is not dated but it stems from the same period as the Ardebil carpet, although some authorities believe it is older, and the knotting is much finer.

### 5 Silk Hunting Carpet (detail)

The hunting designs in one form or another have been a favourite subject in Persian carpets for many centuries, and they are still popular even today. Hunting of course was always a royal pastime, and it was natural therefore that when the court painters were called upon to design carpets they should include this form of sport in their work.

This piece must rank amongst the finest of the world's carpets. Not only are the foundations of silk, but the pile also. Additionally, parts of the figures are brocaded in silver gilt. The weaving is very fine, as one would expect with silk, and it is far closer in weave than any of the other Sefavi carpets.

The size is 22ft. 9in. × 10ft. 7in.

6   7

8

### 6 Animal and Floral Carpet

Another popular subject for Persian carpets is that of animals in combat. Here is one of the finest to have come down to us from the Sefavi period. In the field flowers, large and small, appear to blend in naturally with animals, some fighting, some pursuing their prey, dragons and birds, the combination making what must be one of the most superbly designed carpets of all time. The inner guard border consists of cartouches containing inscriptions praising the carpet and blessing the Shah.

As with all the classic carpets of this period the warps and wefts are of silk, whilst the knotted pile is wool.

Size 24ft. 11in. × 10ft 8in.

20

**7 Animal and Floral Carpet with Medallion**

Although much smaller than the Animal and Floral carpet in the Austrian Museum for Applied Art, the size being 16ft. 7in. × 7ft 11in., this is another fine example of Sefavi weaving in true tradition, with silk foundation and wool pile. In addition, it is embellished with gold and silver brocading. The inscription round the inner border praises the work of the artist who designed the piece, and in the poetic language of the time describes the features of the carpet.

**8 Animal and Tree Carpet with Medallion (detail)**

Here is a detail of one of the most popular designs to have come down to us from the Sefavi period. Half the

carpet is in the Musée des Arts Décoratifs, Paris, the other half being in one of the state museums in Cracow (Krakow) Poland, having lain previously in the cathedral there. The Polish example was restored in 1968. The first mention of the half carpet in the French collection was in the early years of this century. It would appear therefore that the division was made sometime prior to this, although it is not known when, or why it was done. This design has been copied innumerable times, in many different fabrics, and even today it features in one British carpet manufacturer's range.

The size of the Paris fragment (shown here) is 13ft. 5in. × 11ft. 6in. whilst the restored Polish example measures 13ft. 0in. × 11ft. 10in.

**9 The Ambassadors (detail) by Hans Holbein (1497–1543) painted in 1533.**

Fifteen years before this picture was painted, Cardinal Wolsey was demanding 'Damascene' carpets from the Venetian Ambassador in London, and judging by the number of paintings by Italian and Dutch artists in this and the previous century showing carpets in European settings, many indeed must have been imported into Europe. Depending on their designs, some pieces are even today designated as 'Holbein' or 'Lotto' rugs, after the artists who used them.

Of course, not a vestige of any of the original rugs remains as far as is known, but without this pictorial evidence our knowledge of rugs and carpets of these early days would be scanty indeed.

9

# Persia

**10 Isfahan Carpet (detail)**
There is a group of carpets, dating from the late sixteenth or early seventeenth centuries known as 'Vase' carpets, and examples can be seen, mainly in museums. They are attributed to Isfahan. In 1590 Shah Abbas the Great (of the Sefavi dynasty) moved his capital to this beautiful city, where it remained until the middle of the eighteenth century. With the court, it is natural to assume that the carpet manufactory also went, and it is possible that many of the classic Sefavi carpets were woven there.
The example illustrated is typical of the type.
Size 16ft. 0in. × 7ft. 8in.

**11**

**11 Tabriz Carpet (detail)**
The gateway to Persia from north and
west, Tabriz, has always been of
extreme importance, even to the
various conquerors from the eleventh
century, when it was overrun by the
Seljuk Turks. They introduced the
Turkish language, a dialect of which is
spoken there today. It was a capital city
in the Middle Ages, and is still of
course the principal city in the
province of Azerbaijan. The Tabriz
carpets and rugs most prized today
are those of the nineteenth century
revival of Persian weaving, and the
illustration is typical of the fine and
durable work done at that time.
Size 13ft. 2in. × 9ft. 5in.

**12 Polonaise Rug**
This piece is a classical example of the
so-called Polonaise silk, silver and gold
thread rug, which all authorities are
now convinced was made in Persia,
and not Poland as was thought at first.
Dating from the Sefavi period, rugs
and carpets of this nature were given to
royal and other high ranking person-
ages as gifts, particularly to Poland,
Sweden and Russia. Some even have
the recipients' coats of arms on them.
In common with other Sefavi products,
there is no evidence as to exactly where
they were made, but the general
opinion is that they were manufactured
during the reign of Shah Abbas the
Great, possibly in Isfahan.
Size 8ft. 0in. × 4ft. 4in.

Lately in the Kevorkian Foundation
Collection. Sold at Sotheby's,
London, 5 December 1969, Lot 5.

**12**

14

13

**15**

**16**

**13 Tabriz Prayer Rug**
A good example of Tabriz weaving from the end of the nineteenth century. Size 6ft. 3in. × 4ft. 3in.

**14 Tabriz Prayer Rug**
The clear cut appearance of this rather plain design is due not only to the short cropped pile, but also to the fineness of the knotting and the extremely good wool used in the making. Of course, the colours have improved with age, but although today Tabriz can turn out the coarsest of weaves, this picture shows just how excellent were the materials and workmanship in the nineteenth century.
Size 6ft. 0in. × 4ft. 6in.

**15 Tabriz Rug**
Another example of Tabriz weaving in wool. The uneven colouring in the plain field surrounding the medallion is known as *abrash*. It is caused either during the dyeing process when some yarns take the dye better than others, or by the weaver using yarn from a batch dyed at a different time than the original. It is not detrimental to the value of the piece, rather it is regarded as a sign of authenticity, so much so that some machine-made reproductions of Persian designs feature it, although in this type of piece it looks very mechanical indeed.
Size 5ft. 7in. × 4ft. 2in.

**16 Tabriz Silk Rug**
The nineteenth century not only produced some of the finest work in wool from this important centre, many finely woven silk pieces were also made, as the illustration shows.
Size 6ft. 0in. × 4ft. 2in.

## 17 Tabriz Silk Rug

In addition to the skill of the weaver, great credit is due to the art of the designer, and nowhere is this more apparent than in these examples from Tabriz. It was the designer who actually created the piece in the first place, laboriously painting designs on squared paper, one little square for each knot of the carpet. This became the pattern from which the weavers worked.
Size 5ft. 1in. × 4ft. 2in.

## 18 Tabriz Rug

This rug again demonstrates the end product of the combined efforts of designer, colourist, spinner, weaver and finisher, for after weaving, all rugs and carpets must be cropped and washed in local waters.
Size 6ft. 0in. × 4ft. 8in.

## 19 Tabriz Silk Prayer Rug

Here is an interesting example of Tabriz weaving from the late nineteenth century. An unusual feature is the little row of arches above the *mihrab*.
Size 5ft. 0in. × 4ft. 0in.

## 20 Heriz Carpet (detail)

From the small town of Heriz, which lies about fifty miles east of Tabriz, together with its near neighbour Ghorovan, come some of the most easily recognizable of Persian carpets. Chiefly in medallion design on a brick-red ground colour, the curvilinear designs so typical of Persia have no place in the Heriz product. The designs are completely angular, a feature more in keeping with the Caucasus not far away to the north. There is no record of early antiquity in these products, but some very good pieces were made about a hundred years ago. These coarsely woven, colourful but tough carpets made the perfect setting for the oak dining rooms of the West, and even today some good pieces are made.

**21 Heriz Carpet (detail)**
Here is an example of modern work
from Heriz. As will be noticed, the
style does not change, and today it is
one of the few types of Persian carpet
which is kept up to a reasonable stand-
ard, that is, in the better qualities.
Size 15ft. 1in. × 11ft. 7in.

**22 Heriz Silk Rug**
The silk rugs and carpets of Heriz bear
some resemblance in design to those
of Tabriz but they lack the sophistication of the latter, which is not surpris-
ing in view of the difference in the
sizes of these two places. Tabriz could
attract the best artists by virtue of its
importance as a capital city.
In characteristic Heriz colouring, this
finely woven, silk pile rug is a good
example of late nineteenth century
work from this small town. The change
of colouring at the top end of the field
is unusual, but it was done deliberately,
presumably in order to establish the
direction of the piece, which has a one
way design.
Size 6ft. 6in. × 4ft. 5in.

22

**23**

**24**

## 23 Heriz Silk Prayer Rug
This charming prayer rug, not unlike
a Tabriz in appearance, has an added
attraction in the inscription at the
foot of the piece.
Size 6ft 2in. × 3ft. 10in.

## 24 Heriz Silk (details)
Here are two illustrations in close-up
showing details of the intricate
patterns used in the products of Heriz.
*Top* from the field of a silk rug
Size 5ft. 10in. × 4ft. 11in.
*Right* detail of the field of a type of
design which has been popular in
Persia from time immemorial. This is
the 'garden design', where the field is
divided into 'plots' with various
flowers and trees in the sections. It all
creates a glorious illusion of a garden,
to be used in desert areas where there
is a lack of colour, for above all else,
the Persians love all things that grow,
and they are sadly missed in some of
the bleak parts of their country.
Size 12ft. 8in. × 8ft. 4in.

**25 Senneh Rug**
The official name of the home of the Senneh rug is Sanandaj. It is situated in the heart of Persian Kurdistan, not far from the Iraq border. The name of Senneh is well known in the rug world, for this is the name given to the Persian knot, as distinct from the Ghiordes or Turkish knot. This is in spite of the fact that most Senneh rugs are constructed with the Turkish knot, as are all Kurdish weaves. Senneh rugs are very supple, and are extremely finely woven. Also they are cropped very short, giving an appearance completely alien to the other Kurdish weaves, which are of very robust construction. It is indeed strange that this delicate type of rug should be confined to one small town in the vast area known as Kurdistan. The illustration shows one of the best known designs from Senneh. Size 6ft. 5in. × 4ft. 6in.

**26 Senneh Rug**
Another popular design from Senneh, this time in a pine cone or leaf pattern. This particular motif is used extensively in Persia, in one form or another, particularly in Senneh, Kirman and Khorassan.
Size 6ft. 6in. × 4ft. 4in.

**27 Saruk Rug**
Hamadan, the Ecbatana of ancient
times, is the market for the products of
some hundreds of villages in the surrounding neighbourhood, and many
European buying houses have offices
and agencies there. Many of the rugs
and carpets handled are dubbed by the
traders as 'Hamadan', particularly the
long runners of which a large number
are made in this area. Some types of
rug however have separate identities,
and one such type is the Saruk, made
in a small place of that name, but
marketed in Hamadan.
The Saruk rug of the nineteenth
century is a very finely woven and short
cropped piece, and the illustration
shows the resulting clarity of design,
which can only be obtained with fine
yarns, fine knotting and short crop-
ping. The Saruk of today bears little
resemblance to the above description,
but it is very popular in America,
which calls for a very heavy, high
piled, luxurious-looking piece, and
buys it in quantity.
Size 6ft. 5in. × 4ft. 5in.

**28 Saruk Rug**
The wealth of detail in the design of
this fine late nineteenth century piece
can be clearly seen, due to the techniques of the Saruk weavers at that
time. Such rugs are getting more
scarce as time goes by.
Size 6ft. 11in. × 4ft. 6in.

## 29 Zilli-Sultan Rug

Made in the district of Fereghan, these
finely knotted rugs were named after a
person and not a town or village. The
name was really given to the type of
design, of which there are two or three
variations. The rug illustrated is typical
of this nineteenth century production.
Size 6ft. 6in. × 4ft. 4in.

**30**

29

## 30 Bijar Carpet (detail)

Not very far from Sanandaj, home of the finely knotted Senneh rug, lies the small town of Bijar which, together with its surrounding villages, produces what are undoubtedly the heaviest carpets in Persia. Tough, hard, almost like a board, a large Bijar carpet is difficult to handle and it presents problems when it has to be folded for packing. It is strange that such contrasting types of piece should be typical of two neighbouring towns, speaking the same language, using the same basic materials, and observing the same customs.

Size 16ft. 4in. × 10ft. 0in.

## 31 Kashan Rug

'Maksoud of Kashan' is the name woven into the Ardebil carpet in the Victoria and Albert Museum, London, thereby giving this rather untidy city a permanent name in the records of carpet history.

The Ardebil carpet may have been made here, but it is just as likely that Maksoud wove the town name precisely because he was not working there. It is known that textiles were produced in Kashan in the sixteenth and seventeenth centuries, but of course all art in Persia declined after the death of Shah Abbas the Great, until the nineteenth century revival. The wool used in rugs and carpets of Kashan in the latter half of the nineteenth century and into the early days of the present was one of extremely good quality, and this developed a beautiful natural patina, so that when one is seen today, now that the artistically blended colours have mellowed with age, it can be said that here is perfection.

Size 6ft. 8in. × 4ft. 5in.

31

### 34   Kashan Silk Carpet (detail)

As with wool, so did Kashan make some very fine silk carpets and rugs during the nineteenth century revival of the craft.

This illustration shows part of the field design of a medium-sized carpet. The silk and wool products of today from Kashan are however poor in comparison. The materials are inferior to those used in the past, and the designs and colours are monotonous. Occasionally a good piece is made, but it is very expensive when it arrives on the market.
Size 12ft. 2in. × 8ft. 1in.

### 35   Kashan Rug

A further example of the designer's and weaver's skill from the early days of this century—a 'vase' design.
Size 5ft. 3in. × 3ft. 8in.

### 32   Kashan Rug

A good example of the art of the Kashan school of designing. A 'vase' rug, superbly drawn, and finely executed.
Size 6ft. 6in. × 4ft. 6in.

### 33   Kashan Rug

Rather older than the rug in the preceding illustration, the merits of this rug rely on the rich colours and the magnificent wool with which it was made. It is now in the peak of condition and with care will remain so for a long time to come.
Size 6ft. 1in. × 4ft. 4in.

**34**

**36**

**38**

**37**

### 36 Kashan Silk Rug

A tree design in the field, and the main border completely covered with inscriptions. Such a combination of designing skill and calligraphy is not unique, but this particular example shows just how cleverly the two skills can be married when in the hands of the Kashani school.

Size 5ft. 1in. × 3ft. 5in.

### 37 Part Silk Qum Rug

About half-way between Kashan and the capital of Persia – Teheran – lies the town of Qum. It is second only to Meshed as a place of pilgrimage, for here is buried the sister of the eighth Imam of the Moslem faith, and also some Sefavi and Qajar kings. Weaving only started here between the two world wars, as a cottage industry, and some new designs were created by an excellent school of artists. The rugs and carpets were executed in both wool, and wool with some silk in the pile. The illustration shows a piece worked in the latter medium.

Size 7ft. 0in. × 4ft. 10in.

**38 Shiraz Rug (Quashqai)**
The most southerly of the places traditionally associated with carpets, Shiraz is situated in the south-west of the country. It is the capital city of the province of Fars, where most of the so-called Shiraz rugs are made by the tribes of the area, mainly the Quashqais. Another tribe, the Afsharis live in the area between Shiraz and Kirman, and dispose of their products in both markets.

Shiraz conjures up romantic thoughts of rose gardens and poets, and it is indeed a beautiful city, but for our purpose it is only the market place for the surrounding area.
Size 8ft. 6in. × 5ft. 0in.

**39 Bakhtiari Carpet**
The Bakhtiari tribe is one of the largest in Persia, and whilst the majority of its members still live nomadically, a number of them settled in villages something over a century ago in an area west of Isfahan, and it is this section which makes the colourful products known in the markets as Bakhtiari. These are rather coarsely woven, and their rather formal designing belies their nomadic origin.
Size 18ft. 9in. × 11ft. 3in.

39

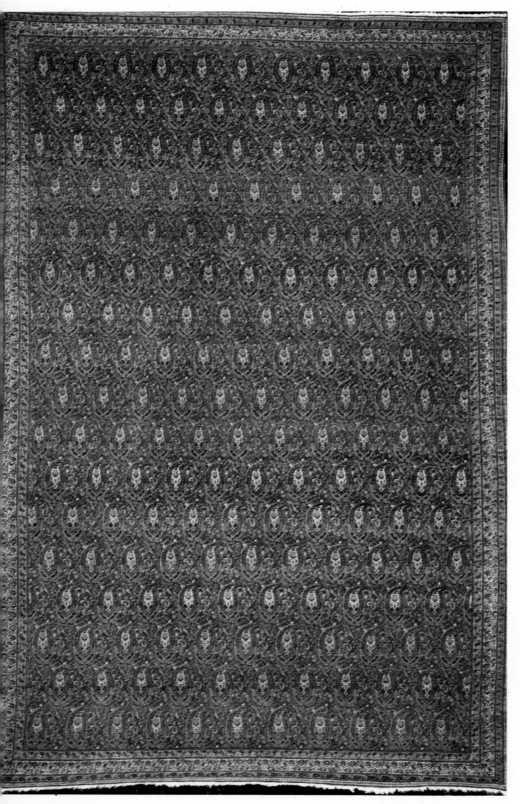

**40**

**40 Laver Kirman Rug**
Made in a small place not far from
Kirman, this rug has the pine cone or
leaf design reminiscent of the earlier
trade in shawls.
Size 6ft. 5in. × 4ft. 2in.

**41 Kirman Carpet (detail)**
This old city, situated on the southern
edge of the desert, which covers a large
portion of central Persia, bears a time-
honoured name in textiles. Rugs and
carpets were being made in the Sefavi
period, even to the extent of exporting
them to India.
With the revival of the craft in the
nineteenth century Kirman became
well known, not for carpets, but in the
making of shawls. These were made in
the pine cone or leaf design, similar to
Kashmir shawls, and also of course to
the Paisley shawls of Scotland. These
latter killed the Eastern market, when
power driven looms and the ability to
print designs became practicable.
When carpet weaving became important again, in the second half of the
nineteenth century the Kirman
products found a market in the West.
Always wonderful designers of floral
motifs, the pieces were closely woven,
of good wool and excellent definition
of design. The present-day, chemically
washed, so called 'American Kirmans'
bear no relationship to the earlier
masterpieces apart from the fact that
they still produce wonderful designs.
Size 15ft. 5in. × 10ft. 2in.

**42 Kirman Carpet (detail)**
A typical example of Kirmani design-
ing of a centre medallion carpet.
Size 13ft. 2in. × 9ft. 9in.

**43 Quashqai Kelleye**
Although small for a Kelleye, this
piece has the right proportions. Made
by the Quashqai tribe in the vicinity of
Shiraz, this colourful example shows
just how intricate a pattern can be
executed by a nomadic people.
Size 10ft. 3in. × 5ft. 3in.

41

42

43

44

**44 Kirman Carpet (detail)**
The older Kirman carpets were very
often made in what in the West would
be termed rather elongated shapes, and
this piece is no exception. It was only
when the Persian suppliers started
making carpets specially for export to
Europe and America, that the more
squarely proportioned sizes made their
appearance, due to the differences in
room sizes between East and West.
This attractive piece, with its inscriptions in the main border, is a good
example of Kirman draughtsmanship
at its best.
Size 14ft. 8in. × 8ft. 11in.

45

### 45 Part Silk Teheran Carpet

Very few pieces are attributed to Teheran, the present capital of Persia, as only a small quantity emanates from there, and those are modern reproductions of the old designs, plus some modern adaptations drawn by local artists. Always very fine in weave, and as the illustration shows, sometimes with a portion of silk in the pile, the modern Teheran appears to be a prestige article rather than a commercial one. However, the city itself is an important market for carpets and rugs from all over the country.
Size 10ft. 4in. × 7ft. 0in.

### 46 Turkbaff Carpet (detail)

These carpets are made in Meshed and they are the better type of piece from this city, being constructed with the Turkish or Ghiordes knot. In fact, the word Turkbaff means 'Turkish

knot'. The ordinary Meshed carpet is not usually a very inspiring sort of piece. In appearance it is lustreless and dark. In contrast, the Turkbaff is lively, well designed and the wool used is excellent, resulting in a very hard wearing carpet.
Size 13ft. 3in. × 9ft. 3in.

### 47 Kirman Carpet (detail)

Another example of nineteenth century production from Kirman.
Size 16ft. 8in. × 11ft. 3in.

### 48 Khorassan Carpet

The province of Khorassan occupies the north-eastern area of Persia bordering on to Russia in the north and Afghanistan in the east. The principal city is Meshed, the country's most important centre of pilgrimage. Here

is the tomb of Imam Riza, who was martyred in the ninth century, and thousands of pilgrims visit the shrine every year. Meshed is the main distribution centre for the carpets of eastern Persia, and today a modern carpet by this name is made in the city.
This Khorassan carpet is a nineteenth century piece, made in one of the villages in the province, and by virtue of its shape was for home use, and not for export. There is a group of antique carpets known as East Persian, the assumption being that they were woven in Herat, now in Afghanistan, but once a Persian city. There is no evidence that this is so, but this city produced many fine artists and calligraphers in what was known as the 'Herat School' in Sefavi times.
Size 9ft. 0in. × 4ft. 10in.

# Turkey-Asia Minor

**49 Manuscript of the Work of Khwadju Kirmani**

Khwadju Kirmani (1281–1352) the poet, was born in Shiraz, southern Persia. The collection of poems from which this manuscript is taken was copied at Baghdad in 1396 AD by the famous calligrapher Mir Ali of Tabriz. The work was illustrated by the painter Djuna id.

**50 Oushak Rug (Lotto)**

The field design of this rug was used many times by medieval artists, and it was obviously in popular demand in the sixteenth and seventeenth centuries. This particular style has been designated 'Lotto' after the Italian artist Lorenzo Lotto (1480–1556) who used it in some of his paintings.

That this design was an early arrival in England is shown by the fact that there is a rug in the possession of His Grace the Duke of Buccleuch showing the same design. Some authorities claim that the latter was made in Turkey, but the fact that the foundations contain flax or hemp (not used in the carpets of Turkey) can only lead one to believe that it was made in England, copied from an imported piece.

Size 8ft. 6in. × 5ft. 4in.

50

49

51

### 51 Oushak Saph – Seventeenth Century

A rare example of an early Turkish, communal prayer carpet. Turkey shares with western Turkestan the practice of producing these unique pieces. They are used on Mosque floors, where they are quite often scattered in quantity. The prayer arches in each of the compartments are called *mihrabs*. Originally this piece had fourteen compartments, seven in each row, but due to damage two were removed. One end border was completely re-woven sometime in the last century. However, the illustration clearly shows the difference between the 'old' and the 'new' work.
Size 16ft. 8in. × 12ft. 4in.

### 52 Oushak Rug – Seventeenth Century

A large proportion of sixteenth and seventeenth century Turkish pieces are attributed to Oushak, although it is by no means certain that they were actually made there. Oushak however, is right in the centre of the carpet making area of Asia Minor, and it is feasible that this small place was an important market at that time. Certainly it is credited with many of the rugs and even large carpets imported into Europe during this period, although at the time they were merely called 'Turkish'. Here is a small example from the latter part of the seventeenth century.
Size 6ft. 9in. × 4ft. 10in.

### 53 Oushak Rug – Seventeenth Century

Another fine example of Oushak weaving.
Size 6ft. 5in. × 4ft. 8in.

52

### 54 Transylvanian Rug

At the end of the nineteenth century, when the Western peoples began to appreciate and study Oriental rugs, a number of pieces appeared on the market from a district of Roumania known as Transylvania. Although it was obvious that they were not made in Europe, this was the name given to them, and it has remained so ever since. It is now generally acknowledged that they were produced in Turkey, somewhere in the district of Oushak, in the sixteenth and seventeenth centuries. Apparently they were used in the churches of Transylvania, which probably accounts for the excellent condition of many of them. How these typical examples of Moslem art found their way into Christian churches has not been satisfactorily explained, but there are some theories advanced which sound feasible enough.
This particular piece is not a typical design. It is a rare example of what is known as the 'column' variety.
Size 6ft. 9in. × 5ft. 3in.

53

55

56

### 55 Ghiordes Prayer Rug

This small town gave its name to one of the two basic knots used to weave Oriental carpets wherever they are made. There are various types of Ghiordes rug, but this illustration is of what is probably the finest weave. It is called a Basra Ghiordes and dates from the seventeenth century. The decoration hanging in the *mihrab* represents a mosque lamp, which helps to give the user a feeling of being in a holy place no matter where the rug is laid.
Size 5ft. 6in. × 4ft. 3in.

### 56 Konia Rug

There is a distinct Caucasian flavour to the design of this rug, which suggests that it was made by weavers imported from the Caucasus, or designed by someone who had been there.
Size 5ft. 5in. × 3ft. 8in.

**57 Ghiordes Prayer Rug**
Another version of the type known as
Basra Ghiordes.
Size 5ft. 9in. × 4ft. 4in.

**58 Konia Prayer Rug**
Until the discovery of the Pazyryk rug,
nearly a quarter of a century ago, the
oldest fragments known were those
exhibited in the Museum of Islamic
Art, Istanbul, and these were found in
the mosque of Ala-ad-din, in Konia.
They are reputed to date from the
thirteenth century, and naturally are
supposed to have been made in Konia,

or at least, in the vicinity. Once the
capital city of Seljuki Turks, this
ancient city was originally known as
Iconium.
The illustration is of a prayer rug from
the early eighteenth century. When
spread on the ground for the purpose
of prayer the *mihrab* is pointed in the
direction of Mecca, the Holy City.
Inside all mosques there is a *mihrab*
built into one of the walls indicating
the right direction.
Size 4ft. 1in. × 3ft 3in.

**59**

**59 Ghiordes Prayer Rug**
Here is a later example of the Ghiordes
weave. The *mihrab* has become rounded, and in the panel above it there are
two inscriptions.
Size 4ft. 4in. × 3ft. 4in.

**60 Ghiordes Rug**
A further kind of Ghiordes rug is
exemplified in these colourful small
pieces, which are always of similar
design to the illustration. They are the
Kiz-Ghiordes rugs of the late eighteenth century. The prefix Kiz means
'maiden' and these rugs were reputedly
woven by young girls as part of their
dowry, or to show their prowess as
weavers to their prospective bride-
grooms.
Size 4ft. 3in. × 3ft. 9in.

**61 Ghiordes Rug**
An unusual example from the looms of
Ghiordes, this rug was made in the
middle of the nineteenth century.
Around this time there was a vogue in
Turkey for furniture and accessories in
the French style, particularly at court,
and amongst high ranking officials and
diplomats. At this time also, Turkey
imported carpets for court use, and
both the Axminster hand knotted factory, and the Wilton factory in England
supplied hand knotted carpets for the
Sultan.
Size 5ft. 10in. × 3ft. 7in.

**60**

62

63

### 62 Koula Rug
Not very far from Ghiordes lies the small town of Koula. It is reputed to have been a weaving centre in the seventeenth and eighteenth centuries. What mainly remains today from this period is a series of prayer rugs, somewhat coarser and less colourful than their contemporaries from Ghiordes. The rug illustrated is of a type known as Mezarlik Koula or 'tomb rug', supposedly used to cover the tombs of high ranking people. The main feature of the Mezarlik rug is the two rows of designs bearing a resemblance to cypress trees, within the centre field. Size 6ft. 9in. × 4ft. 2in.

### 63 Ladik Prayer Rug
There are many places in the Middle East named Laodicea (the modern port in Syria, once known by that name is now called Al Ladhiqiyah), but the Ladik rug is popularly supposed to have been made in or near to the Laodicea (now a ruin) adjacent to the town of Denizli in south west Anatolia. It is by no means certain, but at least this particular Laodicea is in a traditional rug-making area, and it is feasible to suggest that the word Ladik is a corruption of this name. Ladik rugs are rare, always in prayer design, and they feature long-stemmed tulips, normally at the top of the piece, dividing three *mihrabs*. The rug illustrated, from the late eighteenth century, appears to be a 'double ended' prayer rug. The picture has been printed with the single *mihrab* uppermost, but it could equally well have been depicted the other way round. Size 6ft. 7in. × 3ft. 8in.

### 64 Ladik Prayer Rug
A fine example of the Ladik prayer rug, this time with a date. It is 1216 AH which corresponds to the year 1801 AD. Size 6ft. 7in. × 4ft. 3in.

**65 Sivas Silk Rug**
There is no historical significance in the rugs from Sivas. The manufactory flourished in the nineteenth century, when very good copies of Persian and European pieces were made. They command high prices in today's markets, due to the excellence of the materials used and the fine weaving. Almost always made in finely spun wool, there can occasionally be found rugs and carpets of silk, as the illustration shows.
Size 6ft. 5in. × 4ft. 6in.

65

**66 Melas Prayer Rug**
A few miles inland from the Aegean Sea lies the small town of Melas. It has no early history of rug making, but nevertheless, some very colourful specimens have emanated from the cottage industry worked there. The piece illustrated is not of a typical design, being rather one of the rarer examples.
Size 5ft. 9in. × 3ft. 10in.

**67 Melas Rug**
Again not typical, this is one of the few examples of a Melas rug of non-prayer design. Rather coarsely woven in comparison with the Ghiordes rugs, yet these pieces portray a blend of colours and a sophistication of design that would do justice to the finest artists and colourists from the large cities.
Size 5ft. 6in. × 3ft. 4in.

66

67

**68 Hereke Silk Rug**
This small town was the scene of a royal manufactory during the nineteenth century, when some very finely woven pieces were made, from wool as well as silk. Some had a French flavour, whilst others were magnificent copies of traditional Persian designs. Many were given as gifts by the Sultan to high ranking visitors, and most of the crowned heads of Europe possessed at least one rug.
Size 6ft. 0in. × 4ft. 2in.

# Turkey in Europe

**70 Late Sixteenth Century Prayer Rug**

This distinctive class of rug has been described over the years as of Persian court manufacture, having supposedly been made in any one of the towns where the court settled during these war torn years. However, it has recently been revealed that a collection of similar pieces is in the possession of the Top-Kapi Serai in Istanbul, and it is now thought that these exquisite rugs were made there for the use of members of the court. The weavers were most likely to be Persians.
Size 5ft. 5in. × 3ft. 11in.

**71 Feshane Carpet (detail)**

The carpet of which this illustration is a detail, was made at a royal manufactory situated in the environs of Istanbul, in the middle of the nineteenth century, and it copies faithfully the style of the French Savonnerie carpets, then in vogue in Turkey.
Size 14ft. 2in. × 10ft. 2in.

**70**

**69 Hereke Silk Prayer Rug**

Beautifully executed, this extremely fine silk rug has all the beauty one associates with royal manufacture. Obviously designed by a first class artist, who must also have been an expert colourist, and made with top grade materials, it is a perfect example of nineteenth century Hereke workmanship.
Size 5ft. 9in. × 4ft. 1in.

**71**

# The Caucasus

## 72 Daghestan Prayer Rug

Sandwiched between the Black Sea and the Caspian, this area, now Russian, is the home of the pieces made with completely angular designs. There is no organized manufacture as in Persia and Turkey, it is purely a cottage and nomadic industry. Apart from the so-called 'Armenian Dragon' carpets of the fifteenth and sixteenth centuries, there do not appear to be many Caucasian pieces in existence earlier than the second half of the eighteenth century, possibly because all their production was purely functional.

Many nineteenth century prayer rugs are still in use. They are colourful, extremely well made and the materials used are first class, as the country is ideal for breeding the hardy sheep that give the tough springy wool necessary for floor coverings. This prayer rug is from the area in the north east of the country known as Daghestan.
Size 4ft. 7in. × 3ft. 10in.

## 73 Derbend Rug

Of coarser weave than the rugs of neighbouring Daghestan, the Derbend rugs from the city of that name on the Caspian Sea are also more dull in appearance as the example shows.
Size 4ft. 8in. × 3ft. 2in.

**74**

**74 Daghestan Prayer Rug**
The beauty of this rug lies in the
artistic balance of colours which its
creator has been able to achieve, whilst
at the same time filling the piece with
the most exquisite ornament. It is
interesting to note that there are 116
pine cone or *boteh* motifs in the rug,
each one being different to its fellows,
and in addition, the rug manages to
include *mihrab*, comb, animals and
birds, and many small jewel-like
objects in the field and around the
*mihrab*. The rug is very finely woven,
and closely cropped to give wonderful
clarity of design.
Size 6ft. oin. × 3ft. oin.

**75**

**75 Daghestan Prayer Rug**
Most Daghestan rugs are of the prayer
variety, with much ornament in the
field. They are tightly woven, of high
quality wool. This example is typical
of the area.
Size 5ft. 9in. × 3ft. 8in.

### 76 Kuba Carpet
To the south of Daghestan lies Kuba, which with the Shirvan district makes up the largest of the Caucasian weaving areas. Kuba is supposedly the place where the 'Armenian Dragon' carpets were made, but there is no direct evidence to support this view. The illustration shows an eighteenth century piece which was probably made for a good class household, for Kuba is a large trading centre.
Size 12ft. 6in. × 6ft. 2in.

### 77 Lesghi Prayer Rug
These rugs come from an area to the north of Daghestan, inhabited by a tribe known as the Lesghians. A fine example of the acute colour sense of these tribesmen is portrayed in this prayer rug, which, in spite of its primitive design, has a beauty not always matched by more sophisticated pieces.
Size 5ft. 5in. × 3ft. 1in.

### 78 Lesghi Rug
The products of the Lesghian tribesmen are very similar to those of Daghestan, but they tend to use a lot of bright yellow and green, which blend remarkably well.
Size 4ft. 11in. × 3ft. 11in.

### 79 Chichi Rug
Not very far from Kuba the village of Chichi produces some rather attractive and easily recognizable rugs. The chief characteristic of the Chichi rug is the main border treatment consisting of oblique bands alternating with stylized flower heads. Also the field is usually filled to capacity with stylized flower heads.
Size 4ft. 9in. × 3ft. 9in.

78

79

### 80 Chichi Prayer Rug
It is unusual to see a Chichi with prayer design, but here again, the main border is in keeping with all the rugs from this village.
Size 4ft. 10in. × 3ft. 6in.

### 81 Seichur Rug
These rugs come from a small place to the north of Kuba, and although this example is not typical of the make, it has the rose-red colouring in the main motifs with which the Seichur is associated.
Size 4ft. 5in. × 3ft. 3in.

### 82 Shirvan Prayer Rug
Finely woven, and with a short cropped pile, this nineteenth century Shirvan reveals the clarity of design which makes these pieces so attractive and sought after.
Size 4ft. 9in. × 3ft. 5in.

### 83 Shirvan Prayer Rug
A further example of nineteenth century Shirvan weaving.
Size 4ft. 5in. × 3ft. 5in.

80

81

82 83

**84 Shirvan Prayer Rug**
There are comparatively few old
Shirvan prayer rugs still existing from
what must have been quite a large
production. This rug is typical of the
area, with its angular designing,
stylized motifs and the absence of the
pillars which are a feature of the prayer
rugs from Turkey.
Size 5ft. 8in. × 3ft. 6in.

**85 Shirvan Rug**
Occasionally, a piece from a given area
can be identified as coming from a
particular village, or at least that the
design is associated with that village.
Such a piece is this one illustrated here
The village is Perepedil to the north of
Kuba and both the field and border
designs of this example are often used
here. For the purposes of trade, however, the name Shirvan is applied to
such pieces.
Size 9ft. 1in. × 5ft. 1in.

**86 Shirvan Rug and detail**
The large peacock-like figures in the field identify this piece as probably coming from the town of Akstafa in the west of the Shirvan area. Designs, however, are copied over and over again in various parts of the country, and that is another reason for such pieces to be designated Shirvan in the bazaars and markets of the world. Size 8ft. 6in. × 4ft. 7in.

86

87

87 **Kazak Rug**
The south west Caucasus, between Tiflis, the capital of Georgia, and Erevan, the capital of Armenia, is the home of these well known rugs. Many Oriental colourists use green, sometimes not very successfully. In this rug,

89

88

however, the dyer appears to have excelled himself. Remarkably so, in view of the wild region where this piece was made by nomads or at best, village dwellers, who not only produced the woven fabric but the excellent materials with which it is made.
Size 6ft. 6in. × 4ft. 6in.

**88  Kazak Rug**
Another typical piece from the Kazak area, showing once again how successfully the use of green can be employed.
Size 7ft. 7in. × 6ft. 6in.

**89  Kazak Rug**
This piece shows the boldness of the Kazak designing. Some authorities say that the cross denotes that it was made by Armenian weavers, who of course would be Christians, but this has not been authenticated.
Size 6ft. 4in. × 5ft. 1in.

**90**

**91**

**90 Baku (Hile) Rug**
Marketed in the oil town of Baku on
the coast of the Caspian Sea, these rugs
are made in the nearby town of Hile.
This particular type of rug is known as
the 'Boteh Hile' identifying the *boteh*
or pine cone motifs in the field.
Size 9ft. 2in. × 4ft. 4in.

**91 Genje Runner**
These pieces are made in the Kazak
area, and are very similar in weave.
The design illustrated is typical, with
its diagonal stripes.
Size 8ft. 6in. × 3ft. 9in.

**92 Carabagh Kelleye (detail)**
These rare pieces are made in the
south of the Caucasus, near to the
Persian border. Many of the rugs from
this district are made by Armenians,
who, being Christian, date their
products in western style. Also from
here came many pieces woven in the
French style. The example shown is
one of the rare but much sought after
designs featuring parrots.
Size 16ft. 5in. × 6ft. 3in.

**93 Bokhara Rug**
The largest tribe in Western Turkestan
is that of the Tekkes, who inhabit the
border country touching Persia, even
spilling over into the latter, which is
why some so-called Bokhara rugs are

brought to the west through the markets of Persia itself. The illustration
is of a typical rug made by these people.
Size 7ft. 10in. × 4ft. 0in.

**94 Yamout Bokhara Tent Bag**
This is one of the most useful of the
many domestic articles from western
Turkestan – a tent bag, made by the
Yamout tribe. Often these are of
unusually fine work, and in addition to
their value as a receptacle in the home,
they are extremely decorative. The
typical Turkoman colouring adds a
touch of warmth to tent life. Yamout
rugs are also found in Persia, as parts of
this tribe also inhabit the north eastern
part of this country.
Size 4ft. 4in. × 2ft. 6in.

# Western Turkestan

**93**

**94**

**95 Hatchli Bokhara Prayer Rug**
The name Hatchli is given to Turko-man rugs bearing the design of a cross in the field. Reputedly they are used as tent doorways, but some of them, as the illustration shows, have a rather unobtrusive *mihrab*, signifying that they are for prayer use.
Size 5ft. 0in. × 3ft. 11in.

**96 Bokhara Prayer Rug**
A rather unusual rug of prayer design, but showing the unobtrusive form of the Bokhara *mihrab*, probably made by the Salor tribe. The products of the Turkomans have never received the attention they deserve by Western collectors. The reasons for this may be that the country itself is almost un-known; that there is no yardstick for denoting the age of the rugs, and, to the layman at least, there is a certain monotony of design and colour. Certainly the Bokhara design is most easily recognized by everyone, and it has been copied in all manner of fabrics throughout the world. The typical ground colour and the inoffensive small all-over motifs lend themselves to the warm and homely furnishing schemes in the West. They are easily assimilated into almost any period of decoration, and consequently should have an appeal which far outweighs the general knowledge of them.
Size 4ft. 3in. × 3ft. 5in.

**97 Samarkand Rug**
There can be no mistaking the Chinese influence in this beautiful piece of workmanship from Central Asia.
Size 8ft. 8in. × 4ft. 9in.

**98 Samarkand Saph**
A very fine example of a Saph or multiple prayer design from eastern Turkestan, and marketed in Samar-kand. The only other place where such pieces are found is Turkey. This piece is made of wool, but some examples are made in this style with silk pile. The compartments are, of course, much too small for the piece to be used in the conventional way. These runners are used as mosque decoration, and as floor coverings.
Size 13ft. 4in. × 3ft. 7in.

# Eastern Turkestan

97

98

# Egypt-India-Kashmir-China

99

100

**99 Chinese Silk Rug**
This is an unusual example to show of Chinese work; a more obvious one would have been the typical Pekin product of the nineteenth century, before modern techniques and western demands created the so-called 'super-washed Chinese carpet'. However, this piece gives a good idea of the kind of intricate weaving in silk that the Chinese were capable of doing in the last century, and it suggests that they were not newcomers to the scene at the time.
Size 8ft. 3in. × 5ft. 4in.

**100 A Carpet in Miniature**
Woven in wool on a silk foundation, with a small amount of silk in the pile, this is one of the finest examples of carpet knotting ever produced. There are between fifty and fifty two knots per inch each way, making about 2,600 knots to the square inch, a total of almost three million individual knots in the whole piece. It is a scaled-down reproduction, knot for knot, of an original sixteenth century Persian carpet. It was made in Kashmir, probably about the end of the nineteenth or the beginning of the twentieth century.
Size 4ft. 3in. × 1ft. 10in.

**101 Mameluke Carpet from Cairo (detail)**
A late fifteenth or early sixteenth century example from the looms of Cairo. These and the later Turkish inspired designs used after the Ottoman conquest are sometimes erroneously described as 'Syrian' or 'Damascus' carpets.
Size unrecorded.

**102 Agra Carpet (detail)**
The Agra carpets of the nineteenth century, are, along with the Persian Bijar carpets, the heaviest of all the Oriental weaves. This example is typical of the work of this period. Size 14ft. 9in. × 11ft. 3in.

# Acknowledgments

The Publisher wishes to thank the following for supplying photographs for the plates in this book:

*Austrian Museum for Applied Art, Vienna : 5, 6 ; British Museum, London : 49 ; Collezione Pogliaghi, Milan : 101 ; Fratelli Fabbri Editori, Milan : 20 ; Hermitage Museum, Leningrad : 2 ; Musée des Arts Décoratifs, Paris : 8 ; Museo Poldi Pezzoli, Milan : 3, 7 ; National Gallery, London : 9 ; Perez (London) Ltd : 10, 12–19, 21–48, 50–100, 102 ; Sotheby's : 11 ; Victoria and Albert Museum : 1, 4.*